Mauro Giuliani's
120 STUDIES
for
Right Hand Development

Revised and Edited by Paul Brelinsky

CLASSICAL GUITAR STUDY SERIES

Presented here are one hundred twenty studies designed to aid in maximum development of right hand technique. These studies, by the master guitarist, MAURO GIULIANI, constitute an irreplaceable part of the standard study material for classical guitar, and for decades have been used by professionals and students alike.

The fingerings in parentheses are secondary and optional; however, the student will find it beneficial to study these exercises using all plausible right hand fingerings. In performing, the smoothest and most logical fingerings should be used. In practicing, the discipline of creative study is equally important and beneficial.

GIULIANI

120 Studies

4

No. 8

No. 9

No. 10

No. 11

No. 12

No. 13

No. 14

No. 15

No. 16

No. 17

No. 18

No. 19

No. 20

No. 21

6

No. 22

No. 23

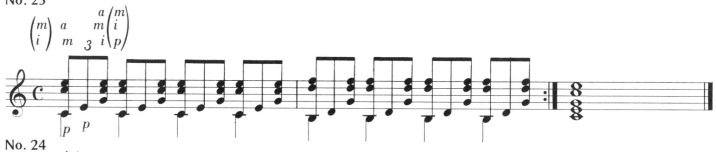

No. 24

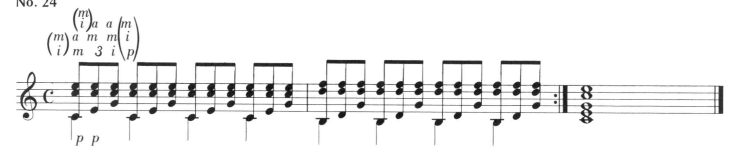

No. 25

No. 26

No. 27

No. 28

No. 29

No. 30

No. 31

No. 32

No. 33

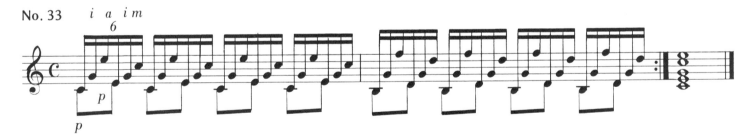

No. 34

No. 35

No. 36

No. 37

No. 38

No. 39

No. 40

No. 41

No. 42

No. 43

No. 44

No. 45

No. 46

No. 47

No. 48

No. 49

10

No. 50

No. 51

No. 52

No. 53

No. 54

No. 55

No. 56

No. 57

No. 58

No. 59

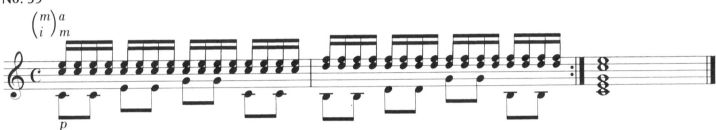

No. 60

No. 61

No. 62

No. 63

12

No. 64

No. 65

No. 66

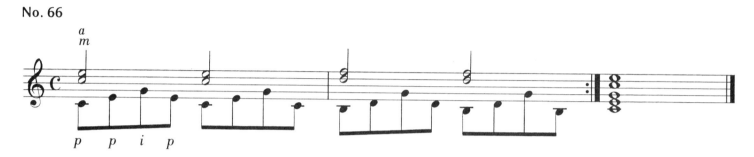

No. 67

No. 68

No. 69

No. 70

No. 71

No. 72

No. 73

No. 74

No. 75

No. 76

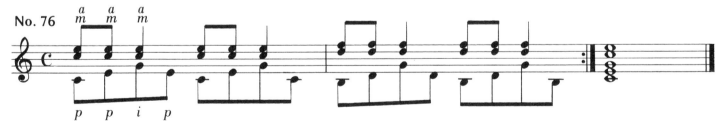

No. 77

14

No. 78

No. 79

No. 80

No. 81

No. 82

No. 83

No. 84

No. 85

No. 86

No. 87

No. 88

No. 89

No. 90

No. 91

No. 92

No. 93

No. 94

No. 95

No. 96

No. 97

No. 98

No. 99

No. 100

No. 101

No. 102

No. 103

No. 104

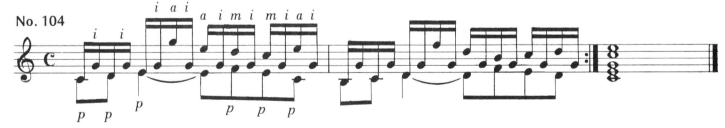

No. 105

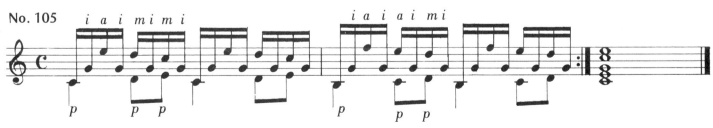

No. 106

No. 107

No. 108

No. 109

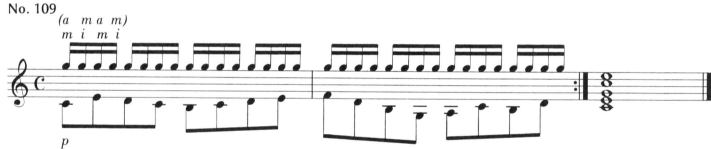

No. 110

No. 111

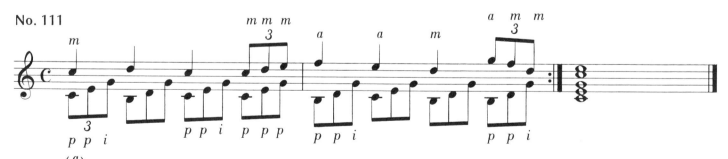

No. 112

No. 113

No. 114

No. 115

No. 116

No. 117

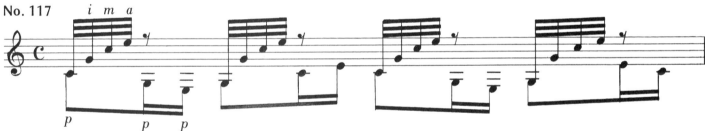

No. 118

No. 119

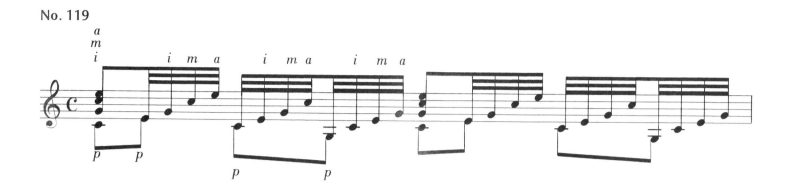

No. 120

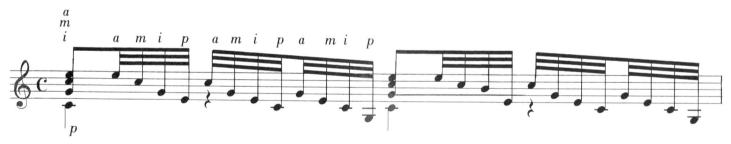